Design: Art of Design
Recipe Photography: Peter Barry
Jacket and Illustration Artwork: Jane Winton, courtesy
of Bernard Thornton Artists, London
Editors: Jillian Stewart and Kate Cranshaw

CLB 3521
Published by Grange Books, an imprint of Grange Books
PLC, The Grange, Grange Yard, London, SE1 3AG
© 1994 CLB Publishing, Godalming, Surrey, England.
Printed and bound in Singapore
Published 1994
ISBN 1-85627-449-7

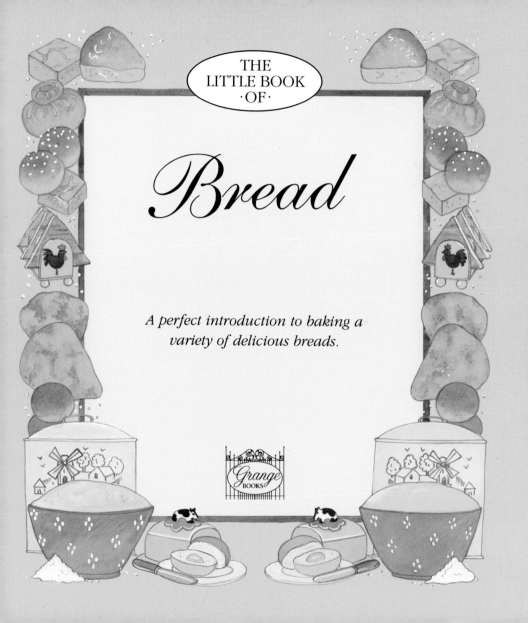

THE LITTLE BOOK ·OF·

Bread

A perfect introduction to baking a variety of delicious breads.

Grange
BOOKS

Introduction

Bread, like rice, is one of the great staple foods of the world. Generally made from wheat flour of one kind or another, it comes in an infinite variety of shapes and sizes. Most of us are familiar with leavened breads – those that are made to rise by the addition of yeast, bicarbonate of soda or baking powder – fashioned into rolls, loaves and sticks. In many countries, such as Greece, Israel and India, unleavened bread is more normal, in which case the bread dough is baked in flat rounds or ovals.

Baking bread is a wonderfully rewarding craft. It is enjoyable to make, smells glorious as it bakes, and can taste far superior to commercially baked varieties. Freshly baked bread, although wonderful eaten on the day it is made, also freezes well and so is suitable for making in large quantities.

The basic process for making leavened bread involves mixing wheat flour with warm water and yeast and then kneading the dough to develop the gluten in the flour. Kneading is the rhythmic pulling and pushing of the dough until it feels sufficiently springy and elastic. The more thoroughly the dough is kneaded, the lighter the finished product will turn out. After kneading, the dough is covered and put aside to rise in a warm place. Yeast responds to warmth by producing carbon dioxide, which forms bubbles in the dough and so causes it to swell. The risen dough is then knocked back and kneaded a little more before being shaped, left to rise a second time, and then baked.

Making unleavened bread is a simpler and quicker process. The dough must still be well kneaded, but once this is achieved all that remains to be done is to roll it out into the required shape and then to cook it. Unleavened bread is not always baked. It is sometimes cooked on a very hot griddle, first on one side and then the other, like a pancake. Chapatties are Indian breads that are cooked in this way, while puris, are deep fried.

The eating of bread is a tremendously varied activity. It can be toasted, enjoyed fresh from the oven with a covering of butter, spread with peanut butter or jam for a quick snack, or filled with countless ingredients as a delicious sandwich.

Unleavened bread is not designed to be sliced, but to be filled or wrapped around other foods. Chapatties are wonderful for wrapping up delicious mouthfuls of spicy curry.

The recipes in this book will provide a tempting introduction to bread making. Try them and you will certainly want to experiment further with the countless varieties available from around the world.

Corn Bread

SERVES 9

This bread is very popular in the Southern states of America.

PREPARATION: 15 mins
COOKING: 25-30 mins

150g/5oz yellow cornmeal
120g/4oz flour
60g/2oz sugar
1 tsp salt
4 tsps baking powder
1 egg, beaten
225ml/8 fl oz milk
30g/1oz vegetable fat, melted

1. Mix the cornmeal, flour, sugar, salt and baking powder in a large bowl.

2. Make a well in the centre and add the egg, milk and melted vegetable fat.

3. Beat very well until the ingredients are thoroughly blended.

4. Pour the batter into a greased square baking tin, and bake in an oven preheated to 200°C/400°F/Gas Mark 6, for 25-30 minutes or until risen and golden brown on top.

5. As a variation, add 30g/1oz grated cheese. Cut into squares to serve.

Boston Brown Bread

MAKES 1 LARGE LOAF OR 4-6 SMALL LOAVES

This is a very different kind of bread, as it is cooked in a tin can! You can add chopped raisins, dates or prunes to the mixture if wished.

PREPARATION: 20 mins
COOKING: 3-4 hrs

225g/8oz fine cornmeal
225g/8oz wholewheat flour
120g/4oz plain flour
Pinch salt
90ml/6 tbsps treacle mixed with 1 tsp
   bicarbonate of soda
420ml/¾ pint cold water
Butter or oil
Boiling water

---

1. Sift the dry ingredients into a large bowl and return the bran to the bowl.

2. Mix the treacle, bicarbonate of soda and water together. Make a well in the centre of the flour and pour in the mixture. Mix just until well blended.

Step 3 Fill the cans with the bread mixture to about two thirds full.

Step 4 Cover the tops of the cans tightly with foil and place on a rack in boiling water to come halfway up the sides.

3. Use a large can from canned tomatoes, coffee or canned fruit, or alternatively, use 4-6 smaller cans. Wash them well and remove the labels, then grease generously. Spoon the bread mixture to come about two thirds of the way up the sides of the cans. Cover the tops of the cans lightly with greased foil and secure with string.

4. Stand them on a rack in a deep saucepan. Pour enough boiling water around the cans to come about halfway up their sides. Allow the water to bubble gently to steam the bread for 3-4 hours in the covered pan.

5. Add more boiling water as necessary during cooking. The bread is cooked when a skewer inserted into the centre of the bread comes out clean. Serve warm with butter or cream cheese.

Naan Bread

MAKES 8

Although naan is traditionally cooked in the Tandoor, a very hot oven will work well, but the distinctive taste of clay cooking will be missing.

PREPARATION: 10-15 mins, plus ¾-1¼ hrs rising time
COOKING: 20-25 mins

460g/1lb plain flour
1 tsp salt
1 tsp Kalonji (onion seeds), optional
1 tsp sugar
1½ sachets fast-action or easy-dissolve yeast
150g/5oz natural yogurt
90ml/3 fl oz lukewarm milk
1 medium egg, beaten
60g/2oz ghee or butter, melted
2 tbsps sesame seeds or white poppy seeds

---

1. Put the flour, salt, kalonji, sugar and yeast into a large bowl and mix well. Reserve 1 tbsp yogurt and add the rest to the milk and blend thoroughly.

2. Add the milk and yogurt mixture, egg and ghee to the flour, knead with your hands or in a food processor until a soft and springy dough is formed.

3. Place the dough in a large oiled plastic food bag and tie up the top so that the dough has enough room to expand.

4. Rinse a metal bowl with hot water and put the bag of dough in it. Put the bowl in a warm place for ½-1 hour, or until the dough has doubled in size. Do not allow the dough to become too warm as this will kill the yeast.

5. Divide the dough into 8 balls, cover them and keep aside for 10-15 minutes.

6. Preheat an oven to 230°C/450°F/Gas Mark 8 and put in an ungreased baking sheet to heat for about 10 minutes. Remove the baking sheet from the oven and line with a greased greaseproof paper or baking parchment.

7. Take one of the balls and stretch it gently with both hands to make a teardrop shape. Lay this on the baking sheet and press it gently to stretch it to about 15-17.5cm/6-7 inches in length, maintaining the teardrop shape. Shape 2-3 at a time and brush with some of the reserved yogurt, then sprinkle with some of the seeds. Bake at the top of the oven for 10-12 minutes, or until puffed and browned.

Quick Home-Made Bread

MAKES 3 LOAVES

The molasses in this recipe gives the bread an attractive appearance.

PREPARATION: 20 mins
COOKING: 35-40 mins

---

1 tbsp molasses
1 tbsp sunflower oil
1.14 litres/2 pints hand hot water
1.5kg/3¼lbs 100% wholemeal flour
2 sachets easy-bake yeast
3 tsps sea salt

---

1. Oil three 900g/2lb bread tins and set aside in a warm place.

2. Add the molasses and oil to half the water, mix and set aside.

3. Place the flour, yeast and salt into a large bowl and mix together thoroughly.

4. Gradually pour the water and molasses mixture into the flour, mixing in with your hands.

5. Add the remaining water bit by bit until the dough is wettish but not sticky. You may not need all the water.

6. Knead the dough about a dozen times, divide the dough between the three tins and press down firmly. Cover with a damp cloth.

7. Leave to rise in a warm place for 5-10 minutes or until the dough has risen near to the top of the tins.

8. Bake in an oven preheated to 220°C/425°F/ Gas Mark 7, for 35-40 minutes or until the loaves sound hollow when tapped underneath.

Puris

The dough for this bread can be made in advance, but rolling out and frying should be done just prior to serving.

PREPARATION: 5-10 mins
COOKING: 15-20 mins

275g/10oz fine wholemeal flour or chapatti flour
½ tsp salt
¼ tsp sugar
15g/½oz margarine
140-280ml/5-10 fl oz warm water (quantity will depend on the texture of the flour)
Oil for deep frying

---

1. In a bowl, mix the flour, salt and sugar. Rub in the margarine. Now slowly add enough of the water, mixing and kneading, to form a stiff dough.

2. Divide the dough into 14-15 equal portions, and roll into balls about 4cm/1½ inches in diameter. Dust each lightly with a little extra flour and flatten into round cakes. Cover them with a damp cloth.

3. Roll out the puris to 9cm/3½-inch diameter discs. Rolling out should be done evenly to ensure tight edges which help the puris to puff up when they are cooked. If they are damaged or pierced they will not puff up.

4. It is easier to roll and fry one puri at a time. Do not stack them on top of each other as they will all stick together.

5. Heat the oil to 160°C/325°F in a deep-fat fryer. Place one puri at a time in the oil and gently press it down with a slotted spoon. As soon as the puri puffs up turn it over and cook for about 30 seconds. Drain on kitchen paper. Fry the remaining puris in the same way.

6. Do not heap the fried puris on top of each other but place them on an open tray so as not to flatten or damage them.

Scofa Bread

MAKES 1 LOAF

This chunky bread is ideal served warm with a ploughman's lunch or a salad.

PREPARATION: 10 mins
COOKING: 1 hr

570g/1¼lbs self-raising wholemeal flour
225g/8oz bran
1 tsp salt
120g/4oz butter or margarine
Just under 570ml/1 pint water
1 tbsp oil

---

1. Put the flour, bran and salt into a mixing bowl.

2. Rub in the butter and mix the water and oil together.

3. Make a well in the centre of the flour and pour in the water and oil.

4. Mix in the flour, gradually drawing it into the liquid mixture from the sides, until a dough is formed.

5. Shape into an 18cm/7-inch round and place on a greased baking tray.

6. With a sharp knife mark into four sections cutting to within 1.25cm/½-inch of the bottom.

7. Bake just above the centre of an oven preheated to 200°C/400°F/Gas Mark 6, for about 1 hour or until nicely browned and 'hollow' sounding when tapped underneath.

8. Remove from the oven and wrap in a clean tea-towel to cool.

Rotis

MAKES 8 Rotis

Rotis are a type of Indian unleavened wholemeal bread. If you cannot get chapatti flour, use equal quantities of wholemeal flour and plain flour.

PREPARATION: 20-25 mins
COOKING: 25-30 mins

½ tsp salt
60g/2oz butter, or ghee
340g/12oz chapatti flour or 160g/6oz each of wholemeal and plain flour
175-280ml/6-10 fl oz warm water (quantity depends on the texture of the flour)
2 tbsps ghee or unsalted butter, for frying

---

1. Rub the salt and fat into the flour until it resembles coarse breadcrumbs.

2. Gradually add the water and knead until a soft and pliable dough is formed. This may be done in a food processor if wished.

3. Divide the dough into 8 round balls. Flatten each between your palms into a round cake and dust it very lightly in a little plain flour.

4. Roll them out to circles about 15cm/6-inch diameter. Cover the rest of the dough with a damp cloth while you are working on one.

5. Heat a heavy-based frying pan over a medium heat. When the pan is hot, place a roti on it and flip it over after about 30 seconds. Spread 1 tsp ghee or butter over it and turn the roti over.

6. Repeat the process for the other side. Brown both sides evenly and remove from heat. Repeat with the remaining rotis.

7. To keep the rotis warm, line a piece of foil with kitchen paper and put the cooked rotis on one half, cover with the other half and seal the edges. This will keep them warm for 30-40 minutes.

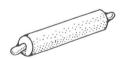

Soft Bread Cakes

MAKES 6

*The bread cakes may be split and toasted, buttered and then filled with cheese
or bacon and fried eggs.*

PREPARATION: 30 mins
COOKING: 15 mins

340g/12oz wholewheat flour
1 tsp salt
30g/1oz fresh yeast
1 tsp brown sugar
1 tea cup of milk
30g/1oz vegetable fat
1 egg, beaten

1. Put the flour and salt in a mixing bowl.

2. Cream the yeast and sugar together until smooth.

3. Warm the milk with the vegetable fat.

4. Mix the milk and fat with the creamed yeast and stir in the beaten egg.

5. Make a well in the flour and work the milk mixture in gradually to make a soft dough.

6. Knead lightly then form into six round cakes.

7. Cover and leave to rise for 20 minutes in a warm place.

8. Bake in an oven preheated to 220°C/425°F/Gas Mark 7, for about 15 minutes.

9. Glaze with beaten egg or milk and sugar a few minutes before removing from the oven.

Sultana Soda Bread

SERVES 6-8

Sultanas add a natural sweetness which makes this bread ideal for serving as a tea-time treat.

PREPARATION: 15 mins
COOKING: 35 mins

460g/1lb plain white flour
1 tsp salt
1 tsp bicarbonate of soda
1 tsp cream of tartar
120g/4oz sultanas
280ml/½ pint sour milk, or fresh milk mixed
   with 1 tbsp natural yogurt

Step 8 Turn the loaf upside down on the baking tray before returning to the oven for a further 10 minutes.

1. Sift together the flour, salt, bicarbonate of soda and cream of tartar into a mixing bowl.

2. Add the sultanas and mix into the flour quickly, making a slight well in the centre of the flour as you do so.

3. Pour the milk into the well in the flour and mix with a round bladed knife to form a firm, but not too stiff dough.

4. Turn the dough onto a lightly floured board and knead quickly to bring all the ingredients together well.

5. Shape the dough into a round and flatten it slightly with the palm of your hand.

6. Place the dough round on a lightly greased and floured baking sheet. Cut a deep cross into the top of the dough with a sharp knife.

7. Bake the dough in an oven preheated to 200°C/400°F/Gas Mark 6, for 25 minutes.

8. After this time, turn the loaf upside down on the tray and return to the oven for a further 10 minutes to dry out completely.

9. Wrap the baked loaf in a damp cloth and place on a wire rack to cool completely.

Step 6 Cut a deep cross into the top of the bread dough using a sharp knife.

Parathas

MAKES 4

A paratha is a crisp, rich unleavened bread. It is rather like making flaky pastry but the method is simpler.

PREPARATION: 30 mins
COOKING: 20 mins

340g/12oz wholemeal flour or chapatti flour
   plus 1 tbsp extra flour for dusting
½ tsp salt
150g/5oz ghee or unsalted butter
120-150ml/4-5 fl oz warm water

---

1. Sift the flour and the salt together then rub in 60g/2oz of the ghee until thoroughly mixed.

2. Gradually pour in the water and knead to a soft and pliable dough.

3. Divide the dough into 4 equal sized balls and flatten them between your palms.

4. Dust each with the extra flour and roll out to 20.5cm/8-inch circles. Spread about 1 tsp of the remaining ghee evenly on each.

5. Roll up each circle until you have tubes about 2.5cm/1-inch wide and 20.5cm/8-inches long. Gently stretch the dough lengthways and then curl the ends inwards in an anti-clockwise direction to resemble backward S's.

6. Now flip the upper halves of each onto the lower halves and flatten. Lightly dust them all over with flour and roll out again until the dough is about 20.5cm/8-inches in diameter and 3mm/⅛-inch in thickness.

7. Melt the remaining ghee and keep aside. Heat a frying pan, preferably a cast iron one, over a medium heat and place one paratha on it. Flip it over after about 30 seconds.

8. Spread on 1 tbsp of the melted ghee and flip it over again. Lower the heat and spread 1 tbsp of the melted ghee on this side as well.

9. Press the paratha gently into the pan, using a fish slice. Flip it over after 1 minute and repeat the pressing action. Cook the second side for 1 minute.

10. Continue to cook both sides evenly until the paratha is uniformly light brown. Cook the remaining parathas in the same way.

Wholewheat Bread

MAKES 2 LOAVES

This very moist bread, which uses no yeast, will last for days. If wished add some caraway seeds to the dough before baking and sprinkle some on top of the loaves to decorate.

PREPARATION: 20 mins
COOKING: 1¼-1½hrs

680g/1½ lbs wholewheat flour
120g/4oz white flour
100g/3½oz porridge oats
60g/2oz bran
175g/6oz pinhead oatmeal
60g/2oz wheatgerm
½ tsp baking powder
½ tsp sea salt
2 eggs, beaten
1.2 litres/2 pints milk

1. Mix all the dry ingredients together in a large bowl and make a well in the centre.

2. Add the eggs and milk to the well in the dry ingredients and gradually incorporate the dry ingredients into the liquid until all is well blended.

3. Spoon into 2 greased 500g/1lb loaf tins and bake in the centre of an oven preheated to 180°C/350°F/Gas Mark 4, for 1¼-1½ hours. When cooked, the loaves should sound hollow when tapped underneath.

4. Turn out of the tins to cool on a wire rack.

Tandoori Rotis

MAKES 8

Tandoori Rotis, like Naan, are traditionally cooked in the Tandoor – a barrel-shaped clay oven which distributes an even and fierce heat. However, they can be cooked in a very hot conventional oven, and taste equally delicious though the flavour will be a bit different.

PREPARATION: 10-15 mins, plus 30-45 mins rising
COOKING: 25 mins

150g/5oz natural yogurt
460g/1lb plain flour
1 tsp sugar
1 tsp baking powder
½ tsp salt
1½ sachets fast-action yeast
15g/½oz ghee or unsalted butter
1 medium egg, beaten
140ml/¼ pint warm milk

---

1. Beat the yogurt until smooth, and set aside.

2. In a large bowl, sift the flour with the sugar, baking powder, salt and yeast. Add ghee and mix thoroughly. Add yogurt and egg and knead well. Use food processor for mixing and kneading, if preferred.

3. Gradually add the warm milk and keep kneading until a smooth and springy dough is formed.

4. Place the dough in a large, oiled plastic food bag and tie up the uppermost part of the bag so that the dough has room to expand.

5. Rinse a large metal bowl with hot water and put the bag of dough in it. Place the bowl in a warm place for ½-¾ hour or until almost doubled in volume.

6. Line a baking sheet with greased greaseproof paper or baking parchment.

7. Divide the dough into 8 equal-sized balls, then flatten them.

8. Dust lightly in a little flour and gently roll them out to 10cm/4-inch discs. Place on the prepared baking sheet.

9. Bake in an oven preheated to 225°C/450°F/ Gas Mark 8, for 10-12 minutes. Turn the rotis over and bake for a further 2 minutes.

Granary Rolls

MAKES 10

For a crisp crust brush the rolls with salted water and sprinkle with cracked wheat before baking.

PREPARATION: 1 hr
COOKING: 15-20 mins

340g/12oz granary flour
1 tsp salt
15g/½oz fresh yeast or 2 tsps dried yeast
1 tsp brown sugar
225ml/8 fl oz warm water
30g/1oz vegetable fat, melted

---

1. Place the flour and salt in a mixing bowl and leave in a warm place.

2. Cream the yeast and sugar together with three-quarters of the warm water.

3. Make a well in the middle of the flour and pour in the yeast mixture.

4. Add the melted fat and mix to a pliable dough, adding the remaining water as necessary.

5. Knead lightly for a minute or two, then cover with a clean damp tea-towel and leave in a warm place until the dough has doubled in size.

6. Knead again for 3-5 minutes and shape into 10 smooth rolls.

7. Place well apart on a floured baking tray, cover and leave in a warm place until the rolls have doubled in size.

8. Bake in the centre of an oven preheated to 220°C/425°F/Gas Mark 7, for 15-20 minutes or until the rolls sound hollow when tapped underneath. Cool on a wire rack.

Batura

SERVES 6

Batura is a leavened bread which is made of plain flour and then deep-fried. The dough is made with natural yogurt and has a soft, velvet-like texture.

PREPARATION: 5-10 mins, plus 45 mins rising
COOKING: 12-15 mins

340g/12oz plain flour
1 tsp salt
2 tsps fast-action or easy-blend yeast
1 egg, beaten
150g/5oz natural yogurt
2-3 tbsps warm water
Oil for deep frying

---

1. Put the flour, salt and yeast in a bowl and mix well. Add the egg, yogurt and water and knead until a soft and pliable dough is formed. Use a food processor if wished.

2. Put the dough in a large oiled plastic bag and tie up the uppermost part of the bag, leaving room for the dough to expand.

3. Put the bag into a metal bowl or saucepan which has been rinsed out in hot water and leave in a warm place for ¾ hour to rise.

4. Remove the dough from the bag and divide it into 6 equal portions. Roll each into a ball then flatten into round cakes.

5. Dust one cake lightly in a little flour and roll out gently to a circle of about 15cm/6-inch diameter.

6. Heat the oil to 180°C/350°F in a deep-fat fryer. Place one batura in the hot oil and fry it for 1 minute; turn it over and fry the other side for a further minute or until it is a rich creamy colour. Drain on kitchen paper.

7. Make and fry all the baturas the same way. It is easier to roll out and fry one batura at a time rather than rolling them all out first.

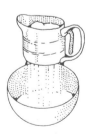

Rich Stollen Bread

MAKES 1 LOAF

This makes an attractive centre-piece on the tea table, particularly at Christmas time.

PREPARATION: 25 mins plus 1¾ hrs proving
COOKING: 30 mins

250g/9oz strong unbleached white flour
Pinch salt
15g/½oz fresh yeast
15g/½oz light muscovado sugar
105ml/3½ fl oz milk, warmed
1 egg, beaten

Filling
1 egg
150g/5oz ground almonds
60g/2oz poppy seeds, plus extra for decoration
60g/2oz raisins, soaked overnight
60g/2oz currants
60g/2oz cherries, chopped
60g/2oz light muscovado sugar, finely ground
30g/1oz dates, chopped
Juice of ½ lemon
Almond essence, to taste

60g/2oz butter
1 egg, beaten to glaze
Flaked almonds

1. Place the flour and salt in a bowl. Cream the yeast and sugar together, add the milk and stir well. Add the beaten egg and leave for a few minutes in a warm place.

2. Add the mixture to the flour and mix. Knead well for 5 minutes. Put into a clean bowl, cover and leave in a warm place for 40 minutes.

3. To make the filling, beat the egg, reserving a little, and add all the other filling ingredients. Mix well – the mixture should be fairly moist.

4. To assemble, knock back the dough and roll out to a rectangle 30.5 × 20.3cm/12 × 8 inches.

5. Working with a short end towards you, dot half the butter over the top two thirds of the dough. Fold the bottom third up then fold down the top to cover. Seal edges and make one quarter turn.

6. Roll out to a rectangle shape again and repeat with the remainder of the butter. Fold over as before but do not roll out. Cover and chill for ½ hour, then roll out as before.

7. Cover with the filling, leaving a tiny margin around the edges. Roll from a short side and tuck in the ends. Place on a baking sheet and brush with the beaten egg.

8. Mark out in 2.5cm/1-inch slices, snipping either side with scissors. Cover with some flaked almonds and poppy seeds and leave to prove for a further 15 minutes. Bake in an oven preheated to 200°C/400°F/Gas Mark 6, for 30 minutes.

Chapatties

MAKES 14

A chapatti is a dry-roasted unleavened bread best eaten as soon as it is cooked. They are not as filling as Rotis or Parathas, so 2-3 chapatties per person is quite normal.

PREPARATION: 20-25 mins, plus ½-1 hr proving
COOKING: 35-40 mins

340g/12oz fine wholemeal flour or atta/chapatti flour
½ tsp salt
15g/½oz butter, or ghee
170-280ml/6-10 fl oz warm water (quantity depends on the texture of the flour)
1 tbsp extra flour in a shallow bowl or plate

---

1. Put the flour and salt in a large bowl and rub in the fat. Gradually add the water and keep mixing and kneading until a soft and pliable dough is formed.

2. Lightly oil the bowl, put in the dough and cover with a damp cloth. Leave to stand for ½-1 hour in a warm place.

3. Divide the dough into 14 pieces and roll into balls. Flatten the balls to make round cakes, then dip each into the extra flour and roll out into discs of about 15cm/6-inch diameter.

4. Heat an iron griddle or heavy-based frying pan over a medium heat and place a chapatti on it, cook for 30 seconds then turn the chapatti over.

5. Cook until brown spots appear on both sides, turning it over frequently. Do not over heat the pan as the chapatties will stick and start to burn.

6. To keep the chapatties warm, line a piece of foil with kitchen paper and place the chapatties on one end, cover with the other end and seal the edges.

Chocolate Cinnamon Sweet Bread

MAKES 1 LOAF

Pull this bread apart to serve in individual pieces rather than slicing it. For a savoury version substitute Parmesan and herbs for sugar and spice.

PREPARATION: 2 hrs, including rising
COOKING: 45-50 mins

Dough
100g/3½oz sugar
1 envelope dried yeast
60ml/4 tbsps warm water
340-400g/12-14oz strong white flour
75g/2½oz butter, softened
5 eggs

Topping
225g/8oz sugar
2 tsps each cinnamon and cocoa
45g/6 tbsps finely chopped nuts
120g/4oz butter, melted

1. Add the yeast and 1 tbsp of the sugar to the water. Leave in a warm place until foaming.

2. Sift 340g/12oz of the flour into a bowl, add the sugar and a pinch of salt. Rub in the butter.

3. Add 2 of the eggs and the yeast mixture, mixing in well. Add the remaining eggs one at a time until the mixture forms a soft, spongy dough. Add the remaining flour as necessary. Knead for 10 minutes on a lightly floured

Step 5 Roll the dough in melted butter and then in the sugar mixture.

surface until smooth and elastic.

4. Place the dough in a greased bowl, cover loosely and put in a warm place for 1-1½ hours or until doubled in bulk.

5. Knock the dough down and knead it again for about 5 minutes. Shape into 5cm/2-inch balls. Mix the topping ingredients together except for the melted butter. Roll the dough in the butter and then the sugar.

6. Layer up the dough balls in a well greased ring mould. Cover and allow to rise again about 15 minutes. Bake in an oven preheated to 180°C/350°F/Gas Mark 4, for about 45-50 minutes. Loosen from the tin and turn out.

Loochis

MAKES 14-15 Loochis

These Indian breads are similar to puris – the main difference is that they are made with plain flour instead of chapatti flour.

PREPARATION: 10-15 mins
COOKING: 15-20 mins

275g/10oz plain flour plus 1 tbsp extra flour for dusting
½ tsp salt
¼ tsp sugar
1 tsp kalonji (onion seeds), optional
1 tbsp butter or ghee
140-175ml/5-6 fl oz warm water (this will depend on the texture of the flour)
Oil for deep frying

---

1. In a large bowl, mix the flour, salt, sugar and kalonji. Rub in the fat and gradually add the water. Knead until a stiff dough is formed.

2. Divide the dough into 14-15 walnut-sized balls. Press them down gently to make flat, 1.25cm/½-inch thick round cakes. Cover with a damp cloth.

3. Dust each flattened cake lightly with extra flour and roll out to about 9cm/3½-inch discs. It is easier to roll out and fry one loochi at a time unless you have someone to help you. If you roll out all of them first, keep in a single layer – otherwise they may stick together.

4. To ensure that the loochis puff up during cooking, roll them out carefully and evenly without damaging or piercing them.

5. Heat the oil to 160°C/325°F in a deep-fat fryer. Place one loochi at a time in the hot oil – it will soon float to the surface and start puffing up. Use a flat perforated spoon to press it down gently on the edge to help it cook evenly. As soon as the loochi puffs up, turn it over gently and cook for about 30 seconds or until lightly browned. Drain on kitchen paper. Fry the rest of the loochis the same way.

6. Keep the fried loochis warm in a hot oven. Spread them out in a single layer so they don't get damaged.

Index